D0627217

BO
CONFIDENTIAL

The Secret Files of America's First Dog

9   8   7   6   5   4   3   2   1
Digit on the right indicates the number of this printing

Library of Congress Control Number: 2009928798

ISBN 978-0-7624-3888-4

Cover illustration: Tom Richmond
Editors: John Ficarra, Charlie Kadau, Dave Croatto & Joe Raiola
Art Direction and Woof Poster: Sam Viviano
Design: Ryan Flanders & Doug Thomson

Running Press Book Publishers
2300 Chestnut Street
Philadelphia, PA 19103-4371

Visit us on the web!
www.runningpress.com

BO
CONFIDENTIAL

The Secret Files of America's First Dog

By Bo Obama
as told to the Editors of MAD Magazine

Illustrations by Tom Richmond

RUNNING PRESS
PHILADELPHIA • LONDON

INTRODUCTION

Hello! My name is Bo Obama. During his campaign, Barack Obama promised to bring a dog to the White House — so here I am! Of course, he also promised to jumpstart the economy, strengthen Social Security, and turn the tide in the Middle East. But, you know... first things first.

I was born in Texas, then moved to Washington D.C., then I lived with a trainer in Virginia, then came BACK to D.C.! Which means that in the first six months of my life, I had four different homes! It also means that I'm already better-traveled than Sarah Palin was when she ran for VP!

The Obamas chose my name, "Bo," in honor of Michelle's dad, who loved Bo Diddley. It's not a great name, but it could've been worse. He could've been a big fan of Gatemouth Brown!

I'm proud of my Portuguese Water Dog heritage! And since I'm a purebred, my birth certificate has been less questioned than Barack's!

So here it is! My first-hand look at what it's like to be the First Dog of the United States. The transition to my new life hasn't been easy. Portuguese Water Dogs are renown for being "brave, loyal and sensible." So, obviously, I don't fit in Washington D.C. at all!

Sincerely,

Bo Saddam Obama

(I don't know what the deal is with this family and middle names!)

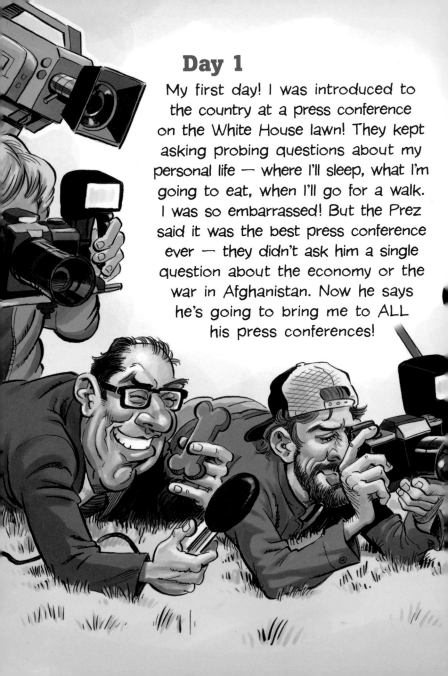

Day 1

My first day! I was introduced to the country at a press conference on the White House lawn! They kept asking probing questions about my personal life — where I'll sleep, what I'm going to eat, when I'll go for a walk. I was so embarrassed! But the Prez said it was the best press conference ever — they didn't ask him a single question about the economy or the war in Afghanistan. Now he says he's going to bring me to ALL his press conferences!

Day 2

The first picture that was released showed me wearing a couple of colorful Hawaiian leis. Oh, great — I've been in the spotlight for two minutes, and I've already got to worry about "gay" rumors!

Day 3

I'm not surprised the Prez went with a dog like me, a Portuguese Water Dog. Of course he'd jump at the opportunity to have somebody in the White House with ears bigger than his!

Day 5

This place is crawling with Secret Service agents. Everywhere you look there are guys with black sunglasses and earpieces. I hear they've all sworn to take a bullet for the President. I don't know what their policy is about guarding me, but I sure could have used their protection when they took me to the vet and lopped off my 'nads!

Day 7

This morning, I met the Vice President,
Joe Biden. What's the deal with his hair?
The last time I saw hair like that, I was
sniffing the butt of a Schnauzer!

Day 9

I've been here only a few days and I've already established my very own Axis of Evil:

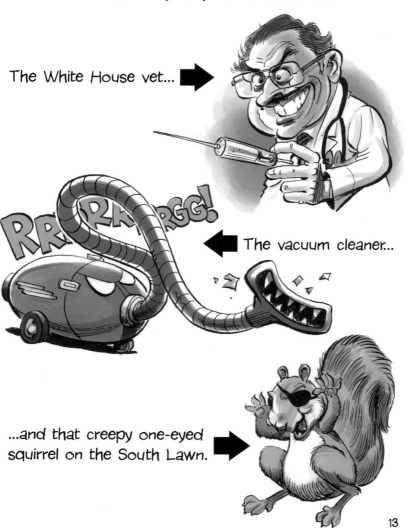

The White House vet...

RRRRARRGG!

The vacuum cleaner...

...and that creepy one-eyed squirrel on the South Lawn.

Things I've learned since arriving at the White House:

#1

The Prez's Blackberry is *not* a chew toy.

Day 10

In the afternoon, Fox News reporter Chris Wallace dropped by to interview the Prez. He was a bit of a jerk, so when he went to pet me, I snapped at him.

I thought I'd be in big trouble...

But later that night, I got steak for dinner.

Day 12

Last night the President put his foot down and told me that I am not allowed to sleep in his bed. That seemed pretty unfair. But then I heard that when they were in the White House, Hillary had the same policy with Bill.

Day 15

I've come to hate taking a walk on the White House grounds. There are no other dog scents to smell!

I'd give anything for a whiff of a tree sprayed by a French Poodle. I long for the delicate bouquet of a fire hydrant where a Pit Bull once lingered.

Sigh.

It's lonely at the top.

19

Day 18

Last night, when everyone was asleep,
I slipped downstairs and sniffed around.
I was overwhelmed by all the historical
greats that have occupied the office.

President Roosevelt's Scottish Terrier, Fala...

President George Bush Sr.'s
Cocker Spaniel, Millie...

President Bill Clinton's Black Lab, Buddy...

The list goes on and on.

How many paws have shaken the hands
of foreign heads of state? How many
antique table legs have been gnawed on?

I get all misty just thinking about it.

God, I love my new home!
Now if I could only find a corner in
this Oval Office to take a whiz...

Day 21

I just found out that I have a chip planted
inside me. They claim it's so that if I'm ever lost,
whoever finds me can return me to The Prez.
Maybe so...but I think the whole thing is a
violation of my civil rights. I'm calling the ACLU.

Day 23

Today the Prez used me to duck some tough questions from the press. When they asked him where his Economic Recovery Plan was, he hemmed and hawed and finally said, "Uhh, my dog ate it." I don't mind being blamed for eating the girls' homework, but there's no way I'm taking a fall for those Treasury stooges, Larry Summers and Tim Geithner!

Day 25

Mrs. O set up a play date for me with Frankie, an FBI bomb-sniffing dog and Jason, a DEA drug-sniffing dog. It was O.K., but all those two wanted to do was talk about sniffing stuff. I mean, c'mon, guys, leave your work at the office!

Day 30

How come the Prez ran on the slogan of "Yes,
We Can," but every time I want to do something,
like play ball with the girls in the Oval Office,
the answer is always "No, You Can't"?!

26

Memo to:
Fed Chairman
Ben Bernanke

From: Bo Obama

Forget GM and
Chrysler — just
make sure *PetSmart*
doesn't go under!
My appetite is too
big for them to fail!

Day 34

This place is huge! There are 132 rooms in the White House and 35 of them are bathrooms.

That's amazing! That means I can go an entire month without drinking from the same toilet twice!

This truly is the greatest country in the world...though someone should remind Robert Gibbs to flush.

Day 38

At noon I met Speaker of the House Nancy Pelosi.
I was a little disappointed. Turns out she's a human.
From everything the Prez's staff had said about her,
I thought she was a female dog.

3 Reasons
Washington is a town full of hypocrites!

① Waterboarding is considered torture, but a choke chain on me is perfectly fine!

② They yell at me if I have an accident on the rug, but whenever some decrepit old senator comes over and does the same thing, no one says a word!

③ At the dinner table I'm not allowed to beg, but the guy from AIG shows up and gets a billion dollars!

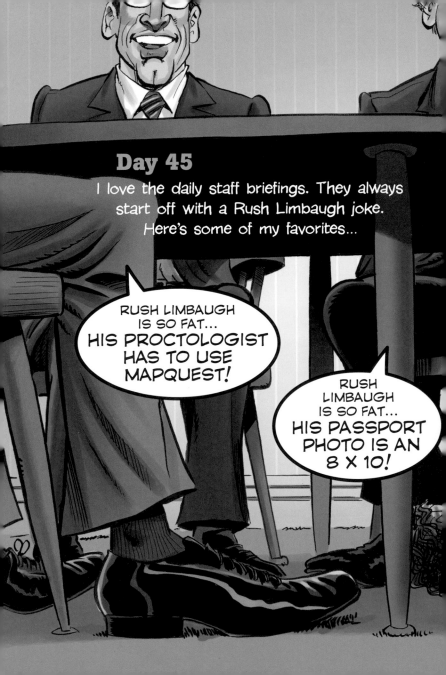

Day 53

Early this morning I needed a walk, so I barked for my master — but nobody came. Just as Hillary Clinton warned during the presidential primaries, Barack Obama wasn't ready for the 3 a.m. call.

Day 60

Even though one human year equals
seven dog years, I STILL don't think
I'll ever be as old as John McCain!

Day 63

I started my day by leaving a turd in an undisclosed location. Next year they'll be finding more than Easter eggs on the White House lawn!

39

Day 64

By my count, there are 319 of those miserable squirrels living illegally on the White House grounds. I figure I'll have to take one out every three days to have them all gone by the time the Prez's first term is over. I just hope I'm not getting myself trapped in a quagmire.

Day 67

Today Mrs. O had Oprah over for lunch. Oprah is such a nice lady! She gave me a box of gourmet doggie treats. And a new car.

Day 68

I just found out that all of the Secret Service agents are heavily armed. Hmm...note to self: When they say "Get off the couch" — get off the couch!!!

Day 70

Whenever I make a public appearance, I like to follow the Prez's lead and use a teleprompter. Sure, we've both been criticized for it, but it helps me stay on message.

Good times! Although, for dogs who are
supposedly experts at detecting things,
they never had a clue when I was bluffing!

Day 77

Mrs. O let it slip to a bunch of school kids that I like to nibble on toes. She really needs to be more careful about what she says from now on. Suddenly my fan mail is full of letters from creepy dudes with foot fetishes!

Things I've learned since arriving at the White House:

#3

Mrs. O gets real mad if you take a nap on anything with a J. Crew label on it.

Day 80

Don't let the name fool you! Portuguese Water Dogs don't know how to swim — we have to be taught. Which is difficult, since it's VERY hard to find floaties, noseplugs and swim caps in our size!

Day 82

Sometimes it really stinks
being the White House dog.

It was beautiful out, but I was stuck
inside all day! Worse still, every time
I looked out the window, I could
see that one-eyed squirrel living
it up and enjoying the weather!

Every day it's the same thing —
I'm cooped up in here, and he's
free to run, climb, jump around —
and taunt me with all the fun he's
having. Any minute now, I expect
him to whip out a tiny Frisbee!

Oh, the humanity.

Day 84

I cannot believe Perez Hilton ran that photo of me licking myself...is there no privacy left in the world???

Day 87

Found out I have worms.

Damn.

And we don't even have
a Surgeon General yet.

Things I've learned since arriving at the White House:

#4

A strategically-placed cold, wet nose can scare the living daylights out of even the most seasoned diplomat.

Day 90

Today a congressional committee came over for an afternoon conference with the Prez. Call me crazy, but I swear that when no one was looking, I saw Rep. Barney Frank snatch one of my biscuits and eat it. That fat load!

Day 92

Here's a funny coincidence — all the newspapers they lay out for me to poop on are ones published by Rupert Murdoch!

Day 95

That news guy Lou Dobbs is such a weirdo. He came over today and kept telling me how, if we don't protect our borders and have stronger immigration laws, I could lose my job to a Mexican Hairless!

Memo to:
The White House Chef

From: Bo Obama

Last night's dinner was superb! Delightfully seasoned, wonderfully presented! I don't know when I've ever tasted more delicious Snausages!

Day 102

This morning I was in the Oval Office when CIA chief Leon Panetta came in to give the Prez the top secret national security briefing.

You wouldn't believe what's really going on in North Korea: ████████████

████████████████████████████

████████████████████████████

████████████████████████████

And in Iraq, ████████████████

████████████████████████████

████████████████████████████

The world is going to the dogs.

Day 104

As I was walking on the south lawn I saw that one-eyed squirrel hold up two acorns and start cackling. If I didn't know any better I'd think he knows about my "procedure." There was something in his expression that said "I have a pair of nuts — do you???"

Day 105

I met "The Dog Whisperer" Cesar Millan today — he got real close to me and whispered right in my ear. I really learned a lot. Namely, that the guy could use about a gallon of mouthwash! Yikes, that's some bad breath! And that's coming from me, someone who routinely eats his own barf!

69

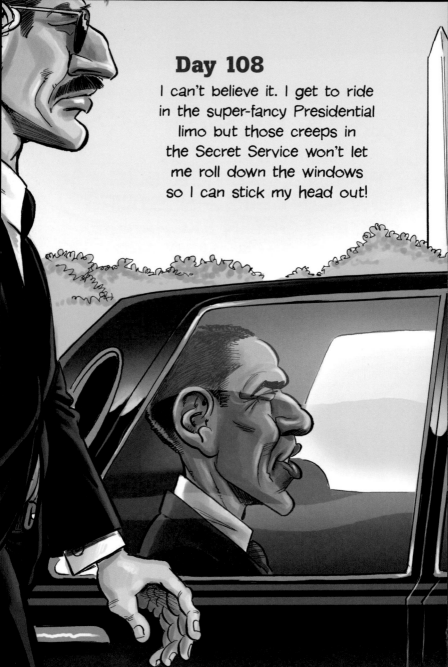

3 *MORE* Reasons
Washington is a town full of hypocrites!

① I have to get distemper shots, yet that hothead Rahm Emanuel storms around the West Wing untreated!

② I catch hell for chasing cars, but those Secret Service guys run alongside the Prez's limo every chance they get!

③ They put that one-eyed mullah terrorist on the FBI's Most Wanted List, but they leave that one-eyed squirrel free to terrorize me!

Day 113

I heard today that the Prez has a 61% approval
rating among the American people. They must not
have asked his mother-in-law, Grandma Marian.
You should hear what she says about him to
Mrs. O when no one is around! (Personally, I don't
agree that Mrs. O could have "done better.")

Day 118

Today we went to Camp David! Nice place, but the minute we got there the Prez threw a stick and told me to go fetch it. Sorry, pal, but I'm not your lackey. Try Chris Matthews.

Things I've learned since arriving at the White House:

Nothing good ever comes from exploring Mrs. O's vegetable garden. Ditto the Prez's Rose Garden. (Just once, I wish this administration would loosen their stance on exploratory drilling.)

Day 120

I'm beginning to hate weekdays.
The Prez and his staff are always so busy
they just ignore me. I have nothing to do.
Now I know how Joe Biden feels.

Day 124

Last night the Supreme Court came over for dinner.
BORING!!! I've met cats that were more interesting.
But the worst was what happened during dessert.
Someone cut one really bad. And right away the
President looks underneath the table and starts
blaming me! What the heck! It wasn't me, it was
Justice Scalia! Him and Clarence Thomas just sat
there snickering. Next time that pompous boob
shows up in the White House, his ankle bone
is in for some cruel and unusual punishment!

Day 127

It occurred to me that the one place George W. Bush didn't look for WMDs was on the White House Grounds. So I've taken it upon myself to dig up the South Lawn and look for them. At least that's my story if the gardener complains — and I'm sticking to it.

Day 130

I gotta get some grooming!
Someone in the press room just
mistook me for Wolf Blitzer!

To-Do List

Write to Secretary of
Defense: Re: Changing the
name of Navy Seals
to Navy Water Dogs

Write to Kennedy Center:
Re: Giving a special
presidential award to the
guy who draws "Marmaduke"

Day 133

I think every person in America who knits has now sent me a sweater to wear. Most are really ugly. But I told Frankie the bomb-sniffer and Jason the drug-sniffer that the sweaters are really bulletproof vests. What's amazing is that they actually believed me. I gotta start hanging out with a smarter class of dogs.

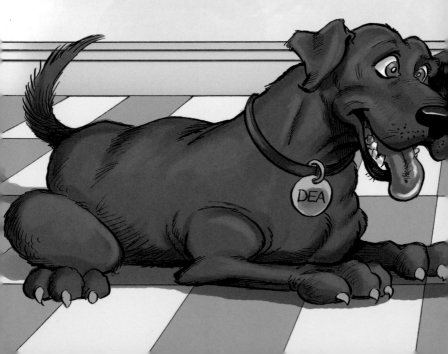

Day 135

Frankie was so fooled by my bulletproof sweater joke, he actually asked if he could have one for himself! I managed not to laugh as I gave him the pinkest, laciest sweater I could find. I told him the frillier it was, the better it would work. Boy, if that were true, this sweater would be indestructible!

Day 139

Not everyone knows this, but the Secret Service gives codenames that all begin with the same letter to the entire first family.

Barack is "Renegade," Michelle is "Renaissance," Malia is "Radiance" and Sasha is "Rosebud." I hated the first one they came up with for me: "Rabies."

Day 143

Bad news — Frankie gave the sweater back. Apparently, his handler didn't think a bomb-sniffling dog should be wearing a fuscia pull-over. Even worse news, the girls found the sweater and thought it was "super cute" — so now I'm stuck wearing this monstrosity! Worst news of all — it's as itchy as it is ugly! Oh my God, I think Frankie gave me fleas!

Things I've learned since arriving at the White House:

#6

The "Don't Ask, Don't Tell" policy does not cover broken vases in the White House

Day 148

Just got word that the Queen of England may be coming for a visit. I can never remember the etiquette — do I rub up against her right leg or her left?

Memo to:
Steven Spielberg,
Dreamworks SKG, Hollywood, CA

From: Bo Obama

Steven,

I have a movie idea I think you're gonna like: The White House is under siege from an interstellar invasion of evil alien cats — everyone is taken hostage, and it's up to the President's dog to save the world from certain annihilation. The black-haired hero dog triumphs, and the alien cats suffer a gruesome, extremely violent demise. Think *Independence Day* meets *Marley and Me*. Get back to me ASAP!

P.S. Vin Diesel has already expressed interest.

Epilogue

Well there you have it — my first report on living in the White House! Looking back, it's clear that life in Washington D.C. is a lot like life in an animal shelter!

- The Republicans and the Democrats fight like cats and dogs.

- Politicians will bark for no reason, even though everyone's telling them to shut up.

- You need to be careful with anyone that gives you a treat — because they'll probably want you to do a trick in return.

- And there's always a snake or two lurking around.

ACKNOWLEDGEMENTS

Authoring a book like this isn't easy —
especially when you only have paws.

I'd like to thank MAD editor John Ficarra, who,
along with editors Dave Croatto, Charlie Kadau and
Joe Raiola, patiently recorded my thoughts and
helped a lot with the punctuation. (My breed is
notoriously weak on comma placement!)

A very special bark goes to Sam Viviano and
Tom Richmond, for envisioning and illustrating
my world — even that #$@% one-eyed squirrel!
Also, thanks to Ryan Flanders and
Doug Thomson for designing a book so
pretty I'd NEVER think of chewing it up!

Finally, thanks to Steve Korte and Emily Ryan Lerner
from MAD Licensed Publishing and Greg Jones
from Running Press. Not only did they help with
this book, but all three came up squeaky clean
in their Secret Service background checks!
They're great Americans!

— Bo